THIS BOOK BELONGS TO

....

Made in the USA
Coppell, TX
04 May 2021

54981126R00063